I THREW MY BROTHER OUT

A Laughable Lineup of Sports Poems

by
TED SCHEU

Photographs by
PETER LOURIE

Young
Poets'
Press

MIDDLEBURY, VT

With thanks: to the brilliant kids, administrators, and teachers at the Edmunds School in Burlington, VT (most especially, librarian Kathy Neil), to a bunch of very smart, photogenic kids in Addison County, Vermont, and also to Tena Bougar of the Mary Johnson After School Program in Middlebury VT, all of whom helped with the project.

Very special thanks to several important people who made this book a reality: Angie Weichmann, editor extraordinaire, for her help in tightening up my words, meanings, and rhythms, and to her youthful associate editor Colt; to my co-conspirator, Pete Lourie—a writer, photographer, and friend of inspiring proportions; and to Win Colwell for his endlessly-clever designs, his patience, and his friendship.

I Threw My Brother Out
First Edition, December 2009

Text copyright © 2009 by Ted Scheu
Photographs copyright © 2009 by Peter Lourie
Design by Winslow Colwell/WColwell Design

Published in the United States by Young Poets' Press
PO Box 564, Middlebury, VT 05753
www.youngpoetspress.com

The text of this publication was set in American Typewriter.

ISBN 978-0-9825499-0-2
Library of Congress Control Number: 2009941865

Come Play!

Whether you throw or dribble or catch
or paddle or pedal or stride,
if you're a runner or a "just-have-funner,"
you're welcome to climb inside.

If you are a leaper with kangaroo sneakers
or a slug who plays slide-and-seek,
please plop or slip or hop or skip
inside for a teeny peek.

You might be a winner or rank beginner
or maybe hate sports—who knows?
Whatever your kind, I'm certain you'll find
some poems that tickle your toes.

This collection is dedicated to kids everywhere who try their best in games and sports, and to their teammates, teachers, coaches, and parents, who inspire and support 'best efforts.'

Table of Contents

I Threw My Brother Out

I threw my brother out today,
and, wow, was he surprised.
He looked at me, and I could see
the sadness in his eyes.

If he had done the same to me,
I know how I'd be feeling.
But I was right to throw him out—
that sneaky kid was *stealing*.

He took a chance and tried to run,
but he was way too late.
He didn't know that I could throw
a ball so strong and straight.

I saw him face the umpire
and start to plead and pout.
But it was clear my throw was there
in time to tag him out.

Swishes

Dribble, stop,
leap, and pop...

Swish!

Alley-oop
to the hoop...

Swish!

Fake and jump,
double pump...

Swish!

All my wishes
end up swishes.

(Or so it seems,
in my dreams.)

Swish!

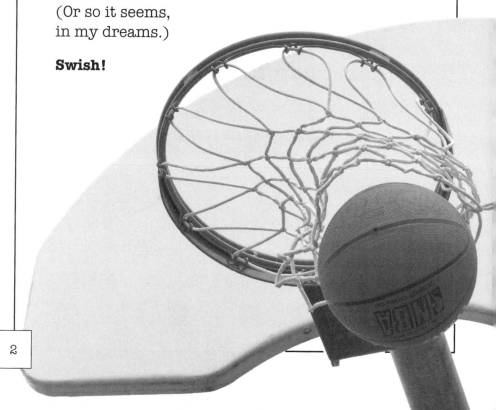

On My Bike

On my bike, I love to fly
around the edges of the sky.
I pull back on my handlebars
and launch myself beyond the stars.

On my bike, I float so free
and swerve around the tallest tree.
I breathe the blue and brush the clouds,
above the roaring roads and crowds.

On my bike, I skid and spin
and flash the birds my biggest grin.
My friends can only gulp and gasp
to see the skill that's in my grasp.

Until it's dark, I never rest.
I put my muscles to the test
and feel the pride inside my chest.
On my bike, I am my best.

I've Given Up

Last night, in what seemed like
the darkest of dreams,
every last one of
my favorite teams—
on their fields and their diamonds,
their tracks and their courts—
lost to the teams
that are worst in their sports.

I've given up watching
and being a fan.
I've got a new hobby,
a passion, a plan.
Sports are too stressful.
I'm glad to be quitting.
I know I'll be happier
sitting here knitting.

I Love PE

I'm a kid who loves PE—
I cannot wait to get there.
My body loves to race and run
and leap and climb and sweat there.

I feel a surge of power when
my body hears a whistle.
It's better than the joy I feel
at recess and dismissal.

My skin begins to tingle, and
my feet begin to dance.
It's almost like my underwear
is full of itchy ants.

One day it might be dodge ball;
the next, a relay race.
If you were there, you couldn't miss
the pleasure on my face.

The love I feel for PE class
is positively scary.
Someday we'll prob'ly get engaged
and maybe even marry.

Hard Landing

I've built a ramp to launch myself
into the summer air.
It's made with boards and dreams and sweat
and a broken-up, thrown-out chair.

My helmet and my feet are set.
My legs and heart are pumping.
And now I'm flying down the hill,
and soon I will be jumping.

I press and push, then leave the earth—
above me all is blue.
I'm upside down and see the ground
and know one thing is true:

My brain has come to realize
a fact I hadn't planned.
It sure was fun to get up here,
but won't be fun to land.

Out Here

Out here
I spit and kick the dirt
and wipe my fingers on my shirt.

Out here
I crouch my body low
and pantomime a practice throw.

Out here
my parents thrill to see
me pound my glove impressively.

Out here
I shout and razz and cheer
and try my best to sound sincere.

Out here
I try extremely hard
to look like I am standing guard.

Out here
I whisper silently
"Oh, *please* don't hit the ball to me."

Ball Dog

My puppy's favorite sport by far
is playing with her ball.
And I'm her go-to, throw-to guy
who's at her beck and call.

She tells me when it's time to go.
I can't ignore her bark.
We grab the ball, her leash, and snacks
and rocket to the park.

Of all the dogs we see, she's best,
and she will let you know it.
She cannot catch to save her life,
but, wow, that pup can throw it.

Gold Medal Kid

Two million eyes are watching me.
One million tongues are cheering.
The fears I might have felt before
are quickly disappearing.

Tonight I'm feeling ready—
completely on my game.
My nerves are cool as arctic ice.
I'm hotter than a flame.

I turn and twist and float and fly
as if my arms were wings.
I rise so high I touch the sky—
my legs are filled with springs.

I scoff and laugh at gravity,
defying all its laws.
With every leap I hear the cheers
and thunderous applause.

Olympic dreams of glory
are soaring in my head,
for I'm the best who ever lived
at bouncing on my bed.

My High-Tech Bike

My bike has got a GPS,
so I will not get lost.
I helped my dad install the thing—
I don't know what it cost.

We also put two webcams on
and split computer screens,
so I can watch my front and back
in multicolor scenes.

My thumbs can play computer games
while I am on my ride.
And in my helmet music blasts
through headphones tucked inside.

Two small electric motors
help me turn and change my gears.
And if I'm tired, I can sleep;
my autopilot steers.

The pride I feel is swelling up—
it's pretty hard to hide it.
And someday soon we'll put on wheels,
and I'll discover how it feels to actually ride it.

Does Your Dog Do?

Does your dog do?
I guess every dog does.
But I sure wish
they wouldn't.

At least not here
on our soccer field.
So if your dog does,
he shouldn't.

Give Me a Hand

I'm not the finest athlete
the world has ever seen.
I'm not a slug or a shooting star—
I'm somewhere in between.

My bottom often warms the bench,
but I don't really mind.
When whistles blow to end the game
it's time for me to shine.

For there's one thing my soccer team
completely understands:
They know when games at last are done—
no matter if we lost or won—
I'm best at shaking hands.

Watching Football

I love to watch a quarterback
launch a pass a mile.
And when that touchdown pass is caught,
it always makes me smile.

It's like a dance when running backs
accelerate and spin.
And if defenders haul them down,
I sneak a little grin.

When helmets crack like thunderclaps,
I feel a teeny thrill.
And every time a touchdown's scored,
my bottom can't sit still.

I watch the highlights on TV
and feel my spirits soaring.
But watch a game from *start* to *end*?
No way—it's much too boring.

Daddy, It's Only a Game

"Deck that kid!
Make him hurt!
Push him down!
Grab his shirt!
Bash the bum!
Make him cry!
Put an elbow
in his eye!
Kick his knee!
Whack his head!
Turn his hair
completely red!"

Daddy, please stop shouting.
Those words are not okay.
They may have worked when you were young,
but I don't play that way.

I'm bursting with embarrassment
and lots and lots of stress.
And Daddy, please remember...
I'm only playing *chess.*

27

Ode to a Hockey Puck

Oh hockey puck,

    your life must stink

inside this frozen

    hockey rink.

From side to side,

    you slide each game—

get no respect

    and less acclaim.

You score a goal

    or even two?

They cheer the players.

    Never you.

With no complaint,

    you take your licks.

You slam off boards,

    get whacked by sticks.

And when the game

    at last is through,

like me, you're always

    black-and-blue.

And lastly, let us

    not forget,

our bottoms both

    are cold and wet.

Standards of Measurement

My father says
it's fifty-two feet
from our front stoop
to the edge of the street.

Sorry, Dad.
We disagree.
It's different for
my friend and me.

> For us, it's twelve-and-a-half giant steps,
> or seventy-one side-footed alien steps,
> or one hundred sixty-two tiptoed baby steps,
> or twenty-two thousand forty-two ladybug steps,
> or eight super-high-speed skips,
> or six pretty-tight cartwheels,
> or five diving somersaults
> that hurt our backs
> when we do it.

It all depends
on how you view it.

Dancing Rules

There was a time when I was sure
that dancing was the *worst*.
I made a list of "Stupid Stuff,"
and dancing was the first.

But now that I have learned some moves,
I find it's pretty cool.
I practice every chance I get,
but never break this rule:

I'll jump and shake and stretch and split
and spin and twist and twirl,
but I will *never, ever, ever,*
ever touch a girl.

When I Want Fun

I don't need a court
or a field or a track
or a cool new shirt
with my name on the back.

I'm fine without sticks
or a ball or a net
or a cute little towel
to wipe away sweat.

Forget about rules
or a ref or a team
or parents who meddle
and coaches who scream.

I say "No way!"
to fancy shoes.
And I don't care
if I win or I lose.

I don't need a buzzer
to beep at the end.
And sometimes I
don't need a friend.

I don't need nothin'
when all is said and done.
When I want fun,
I just *run*.

I Play Great

Inside my new report card,
I found a little note.
I "don't play well with others"
is what my teacher wrote.

I told my parents she is wrong,
as anyone can see.
I play great with **everyone**—
they don't play well with *me*.

Last Kid Picked

When we pick teams at recess
to play a sport or game,
the final sound I'm bound to hear
is when they call my name.

Although I'm always last kid picked,
I'm never sad or hurt.
It gives me time to look for bugs
and doodle in the dirt.

Why Baseball's Better Than Bowling

My friend's in love with bowling,
but I'm a baseball guy.
He says that bowling's best,
but I say no, and here is why:

With baseball, you can run and slide
and do it in the dirt.
And baseball players get to wipe
their fingers on their shirts.

You get to watch the sky fly by,
and sometimes you just sit.
And anytime you want to
you can burp and scratch and spit.

In baseball, if you're losing
and it rains, they'll stop the game.
But when you're inside bowling,
there's so much less to blame.

In baseball, smells surprise my nose—
the gloves, the coach, the sweat.
But best of all, in baseball, strikes
are easier to get.

*Soft***ball?**

They call it
a *soft*ball,
but how
can *that* be?

My head just met
that *soft*ball,
and it
does *not* agree.

Untied

I had the ball with seconds left.
Our soccer game was tied.
I dribbled through the middle, and
I wiggled down the side.

You won't believe what happened next—
I promise I'm not lying.
I took a shot, and suddenly
the ball and my shoe went flying.

The goalie froze for just a blink,
and then she left her feet.
She sprawled and made a brilliant save.
But not the *ball*—my cleat.

While she was down, the soccer ball
continued spinning in.
It crossed the goal as whistles blew
in time for us to win.

I still can hear the cheering
as teammates screamed my name.
I never will forget the day
my shoe untied the game.

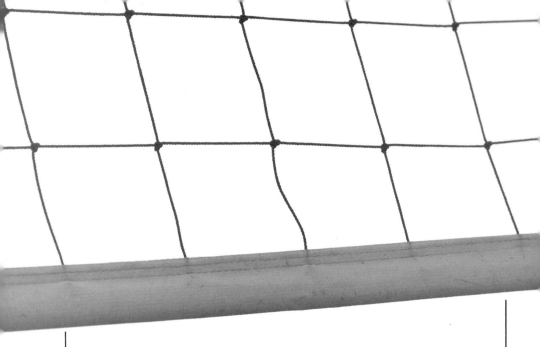

A Very Short Sports Poem

Volleyball,
I'll sadly say,
is silly as
a game can get.

Especially if
you're three feet tall
and you can barely
reach the net.

An Even Shorter Sports Poem

The basketball hoop
is stupidly small
and seventy miles high.

Why?

Foursquare Star

I live for playing foursquare
out at recess every day.
My style is a mixture of
pro football and ballet.

Sometimes I slam the ball so hard,
it rockets to the sky.
And other times my touch gets soft—
like footsteps of a fly.

I dive and leap and slide and stretch
as crowds begin to cheer.
And I can tell by sense of smell
when victory is near.

When I am playing foursquare,
I'm completely in the zone.
I only wish I didn't always
have to play alone.

Communicate!

Our coach will yell "Communicate!"
in games that we are playing.
But with our mouth guards in, it's hard
to know what we are saying.

So each of us got cell phones,
and Coach seems quite perplexed.
We never use our voices now—
instead, we simply text.

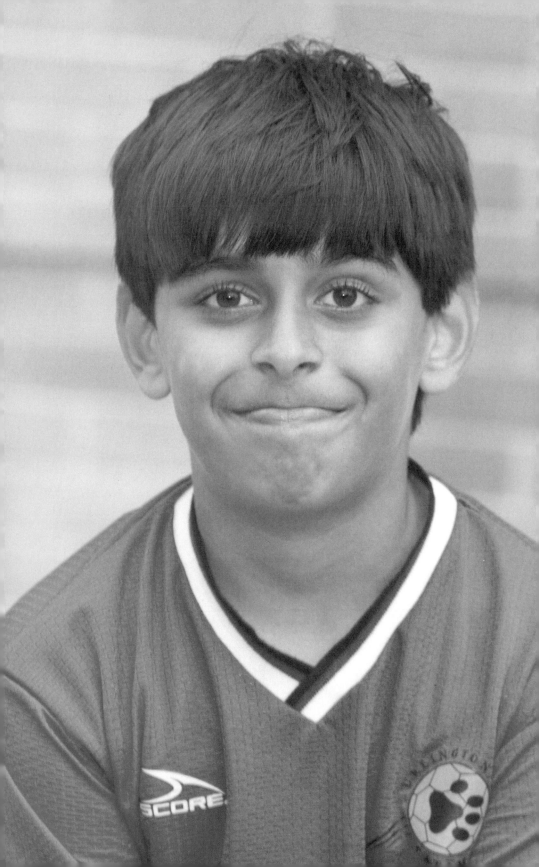

Pull-ups Are Awesome

We had to do pull-ups
this morning in gym.
I knew as I got there,
my chances were slim.

My mouth was a desert.
My fingers were sweaty.
My legs were like rubbery,
soggy spaghetti.

With everyone looking,
I leapt for the bar.
I tugged and I struggled,
but didn't get far.

And just when I thought
I would drop in a pile,
I turned and saw Sally Smith
giggle and smile.

I stopped when I'd counted
to seventy-four.
And I'm pretty certain
I could've done more.

The Perfect Way to Play

In every game, you need to find
the perfect way to play.
I've done this now in many sports,
I'm pretty proud to say.

Take dodge ball, for example—
a game I used to hate.
I use a very simple trick
that's absolutely great:

My friends and I stand right up front—
as close as they permit us.
So when the whistle starts the game,
opponents quickly hit us.

We bravely leave the battlefield
to take a seat, and then
we chit and chat and laugh until
it's time to "play" again.

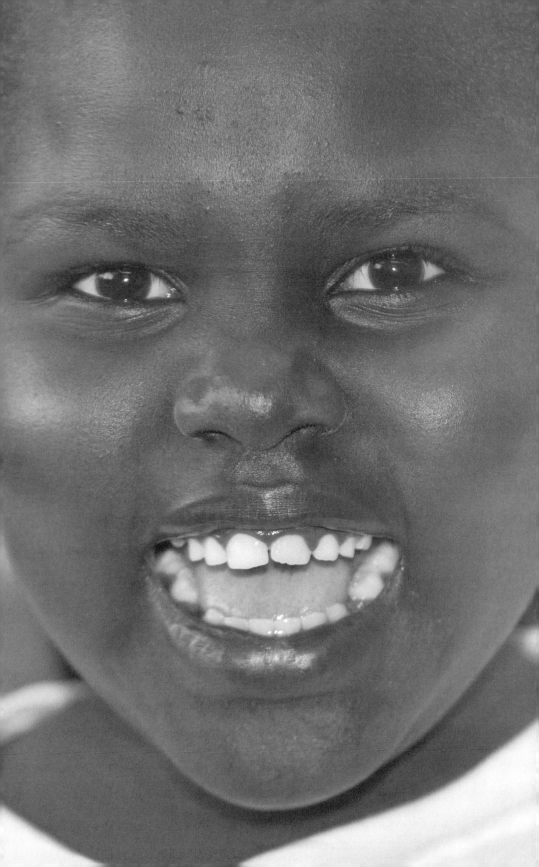

I Never Can Strike Out

Whiff!
"Strike one!"
  It's just begun...

Whiff!
"Strike two!"
  Hey, nothin' new.

Whiff!
"Strike three!"
  Can't disagree.

Whiff!
"Strike four!"
  Who's keeping score?
Whiff!
"Strike five!"
  I'm still alive.

Whiff!
"Strike six!"
(Then seven, eight, nine, ten.)
  Hey, what the heck—
  I'll swing again.

I know someday I'll hit that ball,
then I will dance and shout.
But now I'm glad, when I play with Dad,
I never can strike out.

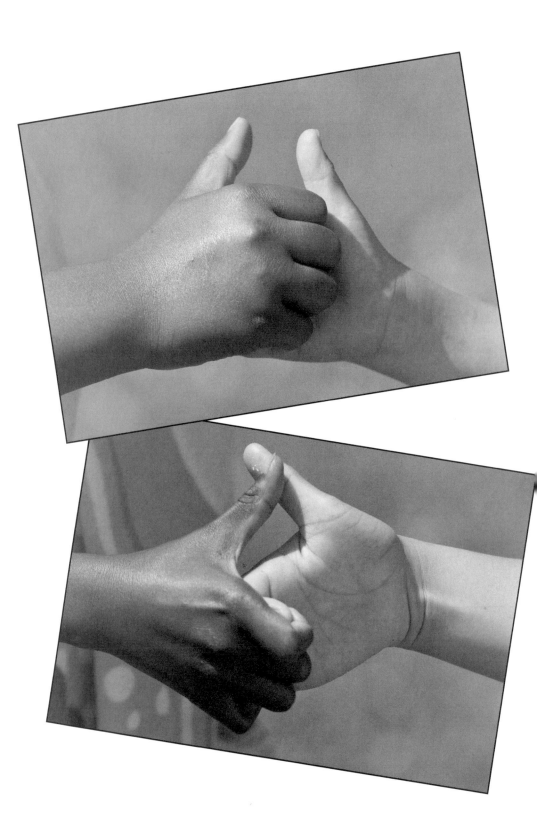

Show Me What You've Got

You ready? I'm ready!
Let's have a little fight.
We'll mix it up—right here, right now—
to prove who's wrong or right.

We'll wrestle hard till one of us
decides he's had enough.
I hope you had your breakfast, kid,
'cause I am feeling tough.

It's way too late to ask advice
from other kids I've fought.
Just grab my hand, stick out your
thumb,
and show me what you've got.

I Love to Lose

Our coach is tough—he yells at us
before our games begin.
His face turns pink and purplish.
He screams, "Go out and *win!*"

When I suggested we should *lose*,
his cheeks turned even redder.
I told him, "Losing's fine because
the other team feels better!

"Winning is just one approach.
It's not the only way.
What if someone on their team
is feeling sad today?

"Our loss will turn a mouth around
and bring a needed smile.
Winning's much too easy, Coach—
losing shows our style!

"So let's go out and lose!" I cheered.
"We'll all feel great! You'll see!"
Well, now I'm on the bench because
my coach did not agree.

I've Never Lost

I've never lost a single game,
I'm very proud to say.
No matter what the sport is,
my trick is *not to play!*

Pretending to Be Brave

Capture the Flag takes quickness
and miles and piles of guts.
And anyone who plays that game
is absolutely nuts.

You have to cross the enemy lines
and race and take a chance.
The only thing it makes me do
is nearly wet my pants.

So I'll just dance along the line
and strike a daring pose.
I'll watch the faster, fearless kids—
and pray the whistle blows.

Bubble Trouble

Today we had a baseball game
that my team should have won.
But the bubble I blew just grew and grew.
It blocked my eyes, the sky, the sun.

So when a ball was hit to me,
I had a pinkish view.
You may have guessed, that bubble was not
the only thing I blew.

Watch Out

I'm a kid who's quiet and sweet—
the meekest kid you'll ever meet,
no doubt.

But when our soccer games begin
and only one team gets to win,
watch out!

Pure Power

My strength is simply staggering;
my courage quite compelling.
And cheers from my admirers
will very soon be swelling.

My mother's mouth and eyes are wide;
she seems completely wowed.
And I can see that she (like me)
is feeling pretty proud.

I'm sure you're also overwhelmed
by my display of power:
I haven't played my video games
for one entire hour!

Batter Up

My palms are sweaty.
Hands are shaky.
Mouth is dry.
And stomach quaky.

My feet are frozen.
Heart is heaving.
Brain is fuzzy.
Unbelieving.

I bet you think that I'm in love,
but it's *much* worse than that...

My team's behind by just a run.
The pitcher's arm is like a gun.
The air is thick with screaming faces.
The count is full, so are the bases.

And I must hit a bullet ball
with this tree trunk of a bat.

Captain for the Day

At gym, the PE teacher made me
captain for the day.
I grabbed my chance and picked my team
a very different way.

The kids who always get picked first
were totally aghast.
I filled my ranks with kids like me
who always get picked last.

The other captain smiled wide;
she understood my game.
So when it was her time to choose,
she picked her team the same.

The athletes were not amused,
but we were on a roll.
For one brief, shining PE class,
the nerds were in control.

It Feels So Good to Cry

My brother says I shouldn't cry
if I get hurt in games.
Criers get teased, he says to me,
and called some wimpy names.

He tells me to "be brave" outside
and also underneath.
He says to just "ignore the pain"
and smile and grit my teeth.

But I do not agree with him,
and I will tell you why:
Inside my heart, when hurting starts,
it feels *so* good to cry.

One Good Thing
(What I'd Love to Say, but Won't)

Stop shouting, Coach. It's clear to me
you think I'm playing wrong.
I do the things you taught me, but
I guess I'm not that strong.

Can't you think of *anything*
I'm doing well today?
I'm sure there must be *one* good thing
that you can think to say?

Say my shirt looks great tucked in.
I don't have breakfast on my chin.
I wear my socks just as I should.
Or when I sweat, the drips look good.

Say you like my curly hair.
I'm super great at breathing air.
Say "Nice try" if I miss the ball
and "That's okay" when I slip and fall.

Say my smile is a winning one.
After all...I am your son.

Speed Freak

I may seem pretty young to you,
but I can really drive.
And even if I crash sometimes,
I usually survive.

I have an endless need for speed
that every day gets greater.
I love to slam my foot down on
that big accelerator.

When driving, I will never be
accused of being lazy,
for I'm the swiftest kid around
at driving my sister crazy.

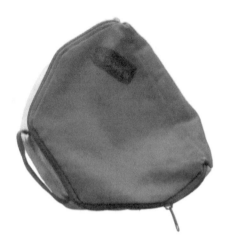

Keep Away

Keep Away is lots of fun,
unless, of course, you are the one
(as I discovered just today)
whose lunch is being kept away.

No-Hitter

It's hard to speak so honestly.
I'm sorry, but it's true:
I've never had a lot of fun
playing games with you.

I bet you think I'm happy when
we hit a baseball hard
and send that thing, with mighty swings,
beyond the neighbor's yard.

I've kept it tight inside me,
but now I must admit
that I'm the kind of baseball bat
who doesn't like to hit.

One-on-One Fun

One-on-one is tons of fun,
and I will never lose.
You can't deny, it looks like I
have rockets in my shoes.

My shot is deadly accurate,
no matter where I fire it.
I get my wish and hear a swish
each time that I desire it.

If you are feeling extra quick,
I challenge you to try me.
No matter how you slide and glide,
you never will get by me.

Your jaw will drop with every pop
in absolute surprise.
And I am *even better* when
I open up my eyes.

What Did He Just Say?

The other team was crushing us,
and we were nearly dead.
Our coach at halftime sat us down,
and this is what he said:

"Your clocks were cleaned out there today!
You guys were freezing cold!
And now you lily-livered wimps
are in a stranglehold!
I've never seen such namby-pamby
pantywaists as you!
We'll have to tip the balance, boys,
and do it PDQ!
This brawl's for all the marbles, men!
It's really do or die!
If we don't get our butts in gear,
we'll all eat humble pie!
It's crunch time, guys! We have to start
to knock upon the door!
If we don't put big numbers up,
we're gonna lose this war!
Pretend when you walk on that field
that you are Genghis Khan!
So dig down deep! Display some heart!
And put your game face on!"

After we'd cheered and howled a lot
and Coach had walked away,
we turned and shrugged and asked ourselves,
"So, what did he just say?"

Soccer Superstar

I'm quite the soccer superstar—
completely in control.
Each time I touch the soccer ball,
I score an easy goal.

I never, ever miss the net,
no matter where I stand.
I always know the ball will go
precisely where I've planned.

I guarantee the shots you'll see
will leave a goalie shaking.
Like fireworks on summer nights,
they're perfectly breathtaking.

Scoring so consistently
for me's an easy feat,
especially when I'm only kicking
acorns down my street.

Pop Flies

When I was out in center field,
I caught a couple flies.
They both came speeding toward my head
and took me by surprise.

The first went *plop* into my glove
and very slightly stung.
The second fly came diving in
and landed on my tongue.

One Fast Fish

At swimming meets, I can't be beat—
I have the strongest strokes.
The other kids, compared to me,
are wet and wrinkled jokes.

To think that you're as fast as me
would be a huge mistake.
I'm guaranteed at any speed
to leave you in my wake.

I'm faster than a tiger shark
who's out to grab some dinner.
Before the starter's signal sounds,
I'm sure I'll be the winner.

In any pool, there's something cool
that makes me even hotter:
I swim each race at record pace
completely underwater.

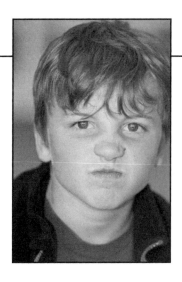

Insulting

Some signs are in our neighborhood—
I've counted two or three—
that have the most insulting words
a kid will ever see.

The folks who put those signs up there
have feeble brains and eyes.
If you come down some summer night,
you'll see those signs are lies.

They say "SLOW CHILDREN" big and bold.
It makes us want to cuss.
'Cause you won't find a bunch of kids
with faster feet than us.

Strongest Team

We're the strongest team in town,
as other teams can tell.
We haven't got the strongest arms—
we've got the strongest smell.

I'm Just a Lonely Goalie

Each soccer game's the same for me:
I stand here in my net
as sad and bored and lonely as
a goalie ought to get.

The problem is, my team's too good,
as anyone can see.
They play each deeply sleepy game
a mile away from me.

I rarely get to make a save
or kick or throw the ball.
Hey, I could do my homework here
or make a cell phone call.

Or maybe I'll just take a nap
and have a lovely dream
that next year I'll be luckier
and join a losing team.

One Sport I'll Never Figure Out

I can attest, I am the best
at every sport I try.
Once I begin, I always win;
I never lose or tie.

I hate to boast, but I'm the most
accomplished athlete
that you (and everyone on earth)
will prob'ly ever meet.

I'm quick as a cricket escaping a net.
I'm strong as a mountain in frosty Tibet.
My throws are like meteors racing through space,
and catching is something my fingers embrace.
I swing like a monkey and climb like one, too.
I fly through the sky like a bolt from the blue.
My kangaroo legs always beg to jump higher.
I'm cool as a glacier and hot as a fire.
I speed like a cheetah that's chasing its dinner.
No matter the contest, I'm always a winner.

That is, until today at school
I tried a different sport.
I nearly cried—I don't know why
my body came up short.

It looked completely simple, but
I know there is no hope.
I'll never learn to sing a song
and jump a stupid rope.

Fast Finisher

I know that I am ready.
I'm sure that I can win.
The other kids cannot believe
the awesome shape I'm in.

My training has been difficult,
but I have met the test.
I may be just a rookie, but
I'm out to beat the best.

The whistle blows—I'm starting slow,
but quickly I adjust.
And soon I'm leaving everyone
exhausted in my dust.

Competitors are slowing now,
and many are conceding.
It's time they crowned the newest king
of power pizza eating!

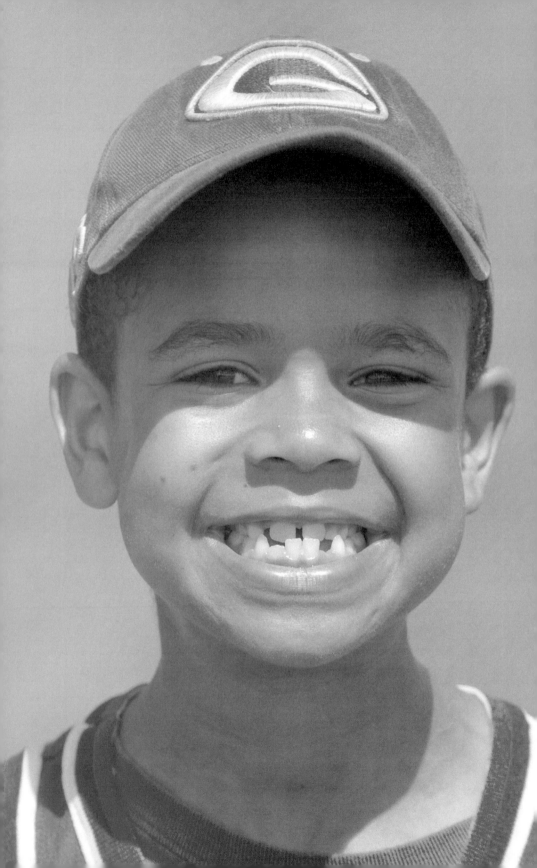

Smarter Than Martin

I'm not as smart as Martin
when we are multiplying.
I'll never be the whiz he is
in science, but I'm trying.

Martin's mind is quicker when
we have to memorize.
I'm pretty sure my brain for that
is just a different size.

We're also very different when
it comes to books and reading.
I slink and slither like a slug,
while Martin's always speeding.

I'm not as keen and confident
at writing things in class.
Martin's words can drive all day,
while mine run out of gas.

Even penning poems,
he's funnier and quicker.
Martin's rhymes get claps and laughs,
and mine might get a snicker.

But when it comes to climbing ropes
and running fast in gym,
Martin knows I'll always be
so much smarter than him.

Thanks to the Team!

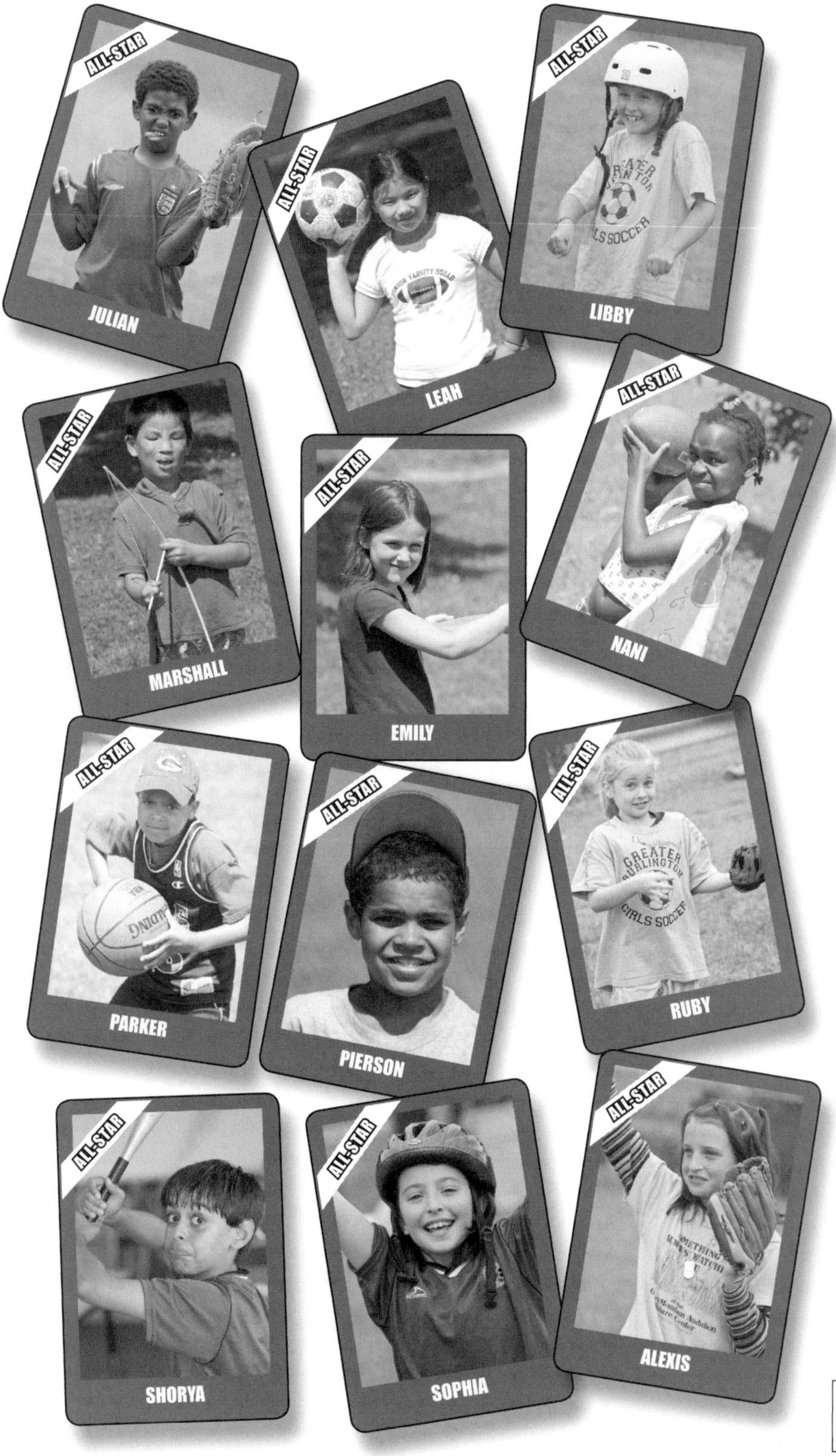

ALL-STAR
JULIAN
ALL-STAR
LEAH
ALL-STAR
LIBBY
ALL-STAR
MARSHALL
ALL-STAR
EMILY
ALL-STAR
NANI
ALL-STAR
PARKER
ALL-STAR
PIERSON
ALL-STAR
RUBY
GREATER BURLINGTON GIRLS SOCCER
ALL-STAR
SHORYA
ALL-STAR
SOPHIA
ALL-STAR
ALEXIS

Ted Scheu
(That Poetry Guy)

TED

Ted has the two best jobs in the solar system: He is totally tickled to be a popular children's poet (who gets to be a kid most every day). And he also loves being a teacher who visits schools and libraries all over the world, sharing his poems and teaching kids to find their own voices in poetry. Ted has been a sports nut all his life—playing them, not just watching them. His favs include bike riding (especially around Vermont where he lives), sailing with friends, cross country skiing, soccer, and laughing. His poems are published widely in anthologies in the US (Philomel, Scholastic, and Meadowbrook Press), in the UK (Macmillan, Scholastic, and Hodder), and in his own collections, "I Froze My Mother," "I Tickled My Teachers," and this new one that you are holding, and also in "Warning! Don't Eat More Than Three! (an audio CD). Learn tons more about Ted at his web site: **www.poetryguy.com**.

Peter Lourie

Peter is an explorer, adventurer, anthropologist, photographer and teacher, and if that's not enough for you, he is also a much-celebrated children's author. In his many award-winning books, he takes you to some of the most remote and rugged regions of the world including the Amazon, the Arctic, and everywhere wild in between. Pete loved the outdoors and playing sports as a youngster (hockey and soccer mostly). And he continues to live a very physical life—often plunging into jungles, traipsing up mountains and following rivers in canoes and kayaks. He is writing three new books for Houghton Mifflin about scientists working with polar bears, bowhead whales, and manatees. Learn more about him at his web site **www.peterlourie.com**. Pete lives in Weybridge, Vermont.

Winslow Colwell

Winslow Colwell is a true renaissance man—a multi-talented designer of books, kites, CDs, T Shirts, and all things design-able, printable, and buildable—many of which may be found at his web site at **www.wcolwell.com**. When he's not using his magic powers to design things, he loves to contra dance with his wife and dance in the kitchen with his daughter. Win and his family live in Ripton, Vermont.

Need more copies of "I Threw My Brother Out" for your favorite 10,000 teammates and family?

1. For super-speedy delivery, go to Ted's web site at **www.poetryguy.com** and push the "Order Books!" link, and you will be zoomed right to the publisher.

2. Fly over to Ted's web site at **www.poetryguy.com**, print out an order form, then snail-mail it to Ted. If you order directly from Ted, he can sign the books for you. Please let him know exactly how you'd like him to inscribe them, when you order.

You may also just send a check by mail for $12.95 (US$) for each book to Ted Scheu, PO Box 564, Middlebury, VT 05753, USA. Please include $3.00 (US) for postage and handling for up to four books, and $3.00 for each four books after that. To order from outside the US, go to #1 above.

3. Or you can surf right over to **amazon.com**, or **barnesandnoble.com**, or **borders.com** and order the book there.

4. Politely ask your wonderful local bookstore order the book for you.

Thanks!